STILLORGAN

Old and New

HUGH ORAM

Order this book online at www.trafford.com
or email orders@trafford.com

Most Trafford titles are also available at major online book retailers.

Print information available on the last page.

ISBN: 978-1-4907-9387-0 (sc)
ISBN: 978-1-4907-9390-0 (e)

Library of Congress Control Number: 2019935243

Trafford rev. 04/29/2019

 www.trafford.com

North America & international
toll-free: 1 888 232 4444 (USA & Canada)
fax: 812 355 4082

ACKNOWLEDGEMENTS

Firstly and most importantly, I should like to thank my dearly beloved wife, Bernadette, for all her loving support for the 40 years that I've been writing books.

I would also like to thank true and steadfast friends who've helped during the production of this book, Thelma Byrne, Dublin; Christina Cannon, Dublin; Aisling Curley, Dublin; Miriam Doyle, Blackrock; Maria Gillen, Athlone and Mary J. Murphy, Caherlistrane, Co. Galway.

For their help in supplying many valuable old photographs, I should especially like to thank Julie Cox of the Beaufield Mews restaurant, Stillorgan; Anne O'Connor and Denis Dowdall of Arklow, Co. Wicklow. Their photographs give especial insights into the old Stillorgan that has long since vanished.

Then, in alphabetical order, I much appreciate all the assistance given by the following people, firms and organisations:

An Óige; Baumanns; Pat Boran, Dedalus Press; brand new retro; CBRE; Veronica Bolay, Stillorgan, for the photograph of her late husband, Peter Jankowsky; Maggie Burns, parish office, St Laurence O'Toole's church; Cramptons; Nigel Curtin of the Lexicon local studies department, part of the Dun Laoghaire-Rathdown county council library service; Larry Dalton, who did the photographs for Bonnie Flanagan's books on Stillorgan; Educational Building Society; Diarmaid Ferriter; Alex Findlater, Cong, Co. Mayo; Gill Books for the photographs of the late Jimmy Magee; Glenalbyn GAA club; Guinness Archives (Arthur Lee Guinness) ; Olivia Hayes for permission to reproduce her watercolours of Stillorgan; Moya Hawthorn for her photograph of Beaufield House in the 1880s; Historical Stillorgan/ Timeline Photos; independent. i.e.; Irish Railway Records Society, Heuston station, Dublin; Kilmacud Crokes GAA Club; Kilmacud Stillorgan Local History Society; Dominic Lee, photographer; Michael Lee of RTÉ for the photographs of the old Stillorgan mansion, The Grange; John Lowe, the Money Doctor, Stillorgan; Brian Mac Aongusa, for his photographs of the site for the Stillorgan shopping centre and the old Stillorgan railway station; Kate McCallion of St John of God' s; Mount Merrion Historical Society; New Island Books and Books Ireland; Maurice Pratt; St Benildus College, Kilmacud; Nevile Shute Norway Foundation; Nimble Fingers; Peadar Ó Riada; Peter Pearson, Co. Wexford; Peter Sobolewski; Stillorgan Village shopping centre; Sunday Business Post; The Irish Times; trip advisor; UCD digital library; Susan Waine for photographs of her father, Jarlath Hayes; Rev Gillian V. Wharton, rector, St Thomas' s; Whytes auctioneers and valuers, Dublin.

Especial thanks are due to Dean Lochner of the Bondi Group in Ballsbridge, Dublin, for all his technical help during the production of this book, including the archiving of all the images. I'm also indebted to Hacketts in Lower Baggot Street, Dublin, for all their assistance in scanning the images for the book.

INTRODUCTION

The history of Stillorgan goes back close on 1, 500 years and it was given its Irish name, Tig Lorcáin, in 900, just over 1, 100 years ago; the present name of Stillorgan is an anglicisation of that name. The church of St Brigid, just over 300 years old and the oldest existing building in the Stillorgan area, has roots that go back just as far, to the days when a monastery became the first settlement in the area.

For many of the intervening centuries since, Stillorgan remained little more than a quiet rural village, sparsely populated, but from the 18th century onwards, the setting for many fine stately homes. The Obelisk, symbol of Stillorgan, and built in 1727, is an ever- present reminder of what Stillorgan was like in its earlier days. By the late 1830s, the Stillorgan area had just over 20 fine mansions.

Some of those stately homes were put to other uses in more recent times, such as Stillorgan Castle, which in 1882, was bought by the St John of God order. It became the basis for the present day hospital campus of the order in Stillorgan. Redesdale House, built in the early 18th century became an industrial school for much of the 20th century. Other great houses in the area were put to other uses, such as St Helen' s, which is now a magnificent luxury hotel just off the main Stillorgan Road.

But until well after the second world war 'Emergency', Stillorgan remained a quiet semi-rural village, with little more than 2, 000 inhabitants. Much of the village centered around The Hill. The old Dublin Road in Stillorgan had many small businesses that today seem quaint; photographs in this book give a good indication was like in Stillorgan in those days. But by the 1960s, much of the farmland that once made up Stillorgan was being transformed into housing estates and since then, the area has become relentlessly built up.

Two new buildings signified a distinct change in Stillorgan' s fortunes and other old photographs in this book show that transformation under way. When the Stillorgan Bowl was opened in 1963, it offered a brand new sporting opportunity, one that was readily seized by the public. It was built on what had been Tigh Lorcáin Farm, once a large farm right in the heart of Stillorgan and one of many farms in the area, now all vanished under bricks and mortar. Three years later came the development of the Stillorgan shopping centre, the first in Ireland, and revitalised in the past couple of years.

To make way for it, many cottages along the old Dublin Road and the Lower Kilmacud Road were demolished, thus speeding the demise of a long traditional way of life in the village. In time, the shopping centre became transformative. During the 1970s, the decade after the shopping centre had opened, much of Lower Kilmacud Road was redeveloped, with many old style homes making way for modern retail outlets.

Since the shopping centre was acquired by an American property company three years ago, it has seen signs of transformation, such as the brand new extension to the Tesco supermarket. What is now the Stillorgan Village shopping centre presents a brighter future for its retailers and their customers. But despite all these changes in Stillorgan, some very long established businesses are still successfully trading today, such as Baumanns, that retailer of endlessly inventive variety, which opened in 1947, and the Nimble Fingers educational toy shop, opened on the opposite side of the old Dublin Road 15 years later.

Leisure time entertainment has also blossomed in Stillorgan, with such pub stalwarts as the Stillorgan Orchard, Boland' s and Ryan' s at Galloping Green, still trading having been in existence in each case since the 19th century. What was once a very circumspect village trade has now developed cosmopolitan wings. The other fascinating development connected with leisure has been the rapid expansion of restaurants. The Beaufield Mews has pride of place, having traded in Stillorgan since 1950, making it arguably the oldest standalone restaurant in the country. Other restaurants have come and gone, like Blake' s and Ping' s, but other eateries like Riba and Aprile' s satisfy collective hunger.

Some famed retailing and catering institutions haven' t survived the passing of the years, like Bewley' s café in the shopping centre, the Monument Creameries' shop on the Lower Kilmacud Road and the Findlater' s supermarket in the shopping centre, but in retail and catering, as in all other walks of life, time moves on as it certainly has done in the case of Stillorgan. Some sites in the heart of Stillorgan have long been derelict and remain to be redeveloped, such as the site of the old Ping' s restaurant and the long derelict Esmonde Motors' garage.

The area has also become noted for its many educational establishments, including Oatlands College, St Benildus College, the Children' s House School and Stillorgan College of Further Education. These establishments have produced a plethora of eminent people, everyone from the late Dermot Morgan, TV comedian to Diarmaid Ferriter, the historian. The wider Stillorgan area has produced many remarkable people, all of whom, in one way or another, have contributed much to the nation' s development.

Dr Thekla Beere was an early pioneer of women' s advancement; Éamonn de Búrca is a renowned antiquarian bookseller; three generations of the Cox family have made and continue to make, a remarkable contribution to the Beaufield restaurant; Denis Devlin was a high flying diplomat and poet; Dave Downes is another antiquarian bookseller; Emer Halpenny has long been teaching drama; Jarlath Hayes was one of Ireland' s leading book designers with an input into the design of Irish euro coins; Peter Jankowsky was a remarkable man, born in Berlin, who made extraordinarily individualistic contributions to so many areas of Ireland' s artistic life; Ossie Kilkenny has long been regarded as the money man to the stars; John Lowe is the renowned 'Money Doctor' ; Séamus P. MacEoin did so much to start the credit union movement both nationally and in Stillorgan; Sir William Orpen, born in Stillorgan, and who became one of Ireland' s leading portrait painters, is being newly honoured with a new sculpture outside the Talbot Hotel; Glen Power, contemporary musician; Séan Ó Riada, who did so much to transform Irish traditional music; Hilda Tweedy, who did so much to advance women' s rights and Dr T. K. Whitaker, who did much to transform Ireland' s economic prospects in the 1960s.

It' s an incredible roll call of talent and people of note from earlier centuries still resonate today, such as Edward Lovett Pearce, the early 18th century architect who designed the Obelisk and the extraordinary Church of Ireland Archbishop Whately. Truly, the present day Stillorgan, urbanised in many ways, is a thriving and varied community, with backed by centuries of storied history, yet constantly reinventing itself in contemporary terms, as this book shows.

The Orchard pub in Stillorgan

Although the single storey pub at the foot of The Hill, opposite the long derelict Esmonde Motors site, is comparatively new, there has been a pub on this site for over 200 years. One picture postcard, dating from about 1908, shows the main street in what was then a tiny village, complete with Cullen's pub and grocery store. In the earlier 20th century, the pub was run by a formidable lady called the Widow Cullen, otherwise Mary Anne Cullen, who married James Boland from the family that owned the nearby Boland's pub. About 15 years ago, plans to call a new bar in the pub after the Widow Cullen came to nothing when her daughter, who lives in Canada, raised objections to the plan.

While the pub began as Cullen's, it subsequently became the Stillorgan Inn, then finally, the Stillorgan Orchard.

In the mid- 1980s, the pub had its biggest ever make- over, when the roof was thatched with over 6, 500 bundles of reeds. At the time, it was said to have been the biggest thatched roof in Europe. When the huge thatched roof was created, the pub was owned and run by the Lavin brothers. In more recent years, Conor and Tony O' Dwyer made many further improvements to the Stillorgan Orchard, but they sold the pub in 2017. It remains a very classy venue, serving all day food and generous helpings of live music.

Boland's pub by the crossroads in Stillorgan village

Boland's pub, at the top of The Hill, where it joins Lower Kilmacud Road, has been trading since the mid- 19th century, some 150 years, making it the oldest pub in the area. Until the middle of the 20th century, the pub was accompanied by a grocery shop, the usual practice in those far off times. In the late 1960s, the last of the public water pumps in Stillorgan village, very close to Boland's, was demolished.

Earlier in the 20th century, three of its most famous customers were writers Brian Ó Nuallain, Maurice Walsh and Brendan Behan. In the 1940s, two of the most famous characters in Dublin were Jack Doyle, a boxer known as the Gorgeous Gael and his Mexican film star wife, Movita. Jack Doyle was one of the regulars at Boland's. In recent years, the pub has had various changes of ownership, the most recent in the summer of 2017, when it was sold for over €1. 4 million.

After one change of ownership, in 2009, the name of the pub was changed to McGowan' s, but the name never caught on and people continued to call it what they had always called the pub, Boland's.

Robert Tweedy with an old-fashioned weighing scales

In 1962, Robert Tweedy, who had run the Court Laundry in Dublin for many years, and his wife, Hilda Tweedy, an early advocate of women's rights in Ireland, set up the Nimble Fingers shop in Stillorgan to sell educational toys for children. At that stage, Hilda was very involved with the Irish Housewives Association, which she had helped set up in 1941 and which lasted until 1992. She played a key early role in the advancement of women's rights in Ireland. The marriage bar in the civil service, not abolished until 1973, meant that she couldn't work in the public service. But she did teach mathematics for many years, from 1962 until 1982, at Alexandra College. Despite all these other involvements, the shop that Robert and Hilda set up became an immediate success and they continued to own and run it for 20 years.

The shop was part of a row of shops known as the 'shopping centre' before the infinitely larger Stillorgan shopping centre opened on the other side of the old Dublin road, in 1966. The Stillorgan Bowl opened at the back of the shop in 1963.

This early photograph shows Robert Tweedy in the then newly opened shop, using an old fashioned weighing scales, to weigh out some sweets.

After Robert and Hilda retired, they lived in a secluded bungalow on Church Road, near St Brigid' s church. The site is now occupied by an HSE building. But in their old age, their existence was cruelly punctuated by break- ins and robberies carried out by local hooligans. In his old age, Robert became both deaf and blind. He and Hilda died within a short time of each other in the same year, 2005.

Robert and Hilda Tweedy, founders of Nimble Fingers

Hilda Tweedy was the daughter of the Church of Ireland rector in Clones, Co Monaghan, where she was born in 1911. In 1929, she joined her parents at Alexandria in Egypt, where her father had been made rector of a local Anglican church. In Alexandria, Hilda did an external degree course from the University of London, although she never completed that course. She and her sister also ran a small school in Alexandria for English- speaking children. In 1936, she married Robert Massy Tweedy. After they got married, they returned to Ireland, where Robert ran a laundry for many years and Hilda got involved in many campaigns to bring about improvements in women' s rights, as women were severely discriminated against.

Stillorgan Bowling Alley

In 1963, a sign pointed to the brand new Stillorgan bowling alley, opened that year, immediately behind the Nimble Fingers shop. The new bowling alley was an instant hit with people from all over Ireland seeking a new kind of sport that had previously only been played in the US. The bowling alley was built on land that was formerly part of the Tigh Lorcáin farm. Over the past 10 years, the bowling alley that became known as Leisureplex, was the subject of various development plans and it was also sold a number of times. In 2016, the Leisureplex complex, which had been owned by Treasury Holdings, was bought for €15 million by Kennedy Wilson, the American owners of the Stillorgan Village shopping centre, on the far side of the old Dublin Road. A substantial development of the site is expected and there are hopes that eventually, the two sites can be linked, across the old Dublin Road.

Nevile Shute

Nevile Shute Norway, to give him his full name, was one of the world's best selling novelists in the 1950s, but in his younger days, he had a close connection with Stillorgan. He was born in London in 1899 and before the first world war, his father had been made head of the post office in Ireland, based at the GPO in Dublin. The family bought a house at South Hill, off Mount Merrion Avenue and close to Stillorgan village.

Nevile Shute's father was in the GPO when the Easter Rising started on Easter Monday, 1916, and within days, the young Nevile, aged 17, began acting as a stretcher bearer for the St John's Ambulance Brigade, tending to combatants from both sides who had been injured in the fighting. In due course, Nevile returned to England, where he completed his studies, at Oxford University. Uin the 1920s and 1930s, before he became a best selling novelist, he worked as an aeronautical engineer. He spent the last few years of his life in Australia; his most famous novel was A Town Called Alice, first published in 1956. He died in Melbourne in 1960.

Arthur Lee Guinness (1797-1863)

A grandson of the founder of the Guinness brewery in Dublin in 1759, Arthur Lee Guinness took £12, 000 out of the family business in 1839 to buy a vast house in Stillorgan, Stillorgan Park, long since demolished. The house itself was notable and Arthur Lee Guinness embellished it with many decorative items and splendid interior décor. The house also had extensive gardens; he was a great proponent of the Irish harp, and weather permitting, he had a blind harpist perform in the garden each afternoon. It's said that the decision by Guinness to use the harp as its trade mark symbol, which began in 1862, stemmed from Arthur Lee Guinness's love of the harp.

But his time at Stillorgan Park was comparatively short lived; he left in 1860 and moved to Roundwood, Co Wicklow, where he died three years later. During his time in Stillorgan, this member of the Guinness family had been renowned for the way in which he helped alleviate the widespread poverty and unemployment among ordinary people in Stillorgan, the ones who didn't live in the big houses. Over 200 local people were employed on the Stillorgan Park estate and he also gave financial assistance to many poor people in Stillorgan.

*Thekla Beere is seen here, third from left, front row, at the opening of
the An Óige youth hostel in Killaloe, Co Clare, in 1956*

Thekla Beere, a remarkable woman who did much to advance equality in the public service, lived at Glenalbyn Road in Stillorgan for many years. Born in 1901 at Streete, Co Westmeath, where her father was Church of Ireland rector, she was one of the first generation of women to graduate from Trinity College, Dublin. Her early career included being the first female lecturer on statistics in Ireland; she subsequently joined the public service and when in 1959 she was made secretary of what was then the Department of Transport and Power, it was the first time that a woman had been made secretary of a government department. Her expertise on transport and labour issues proved exceptionally useful.

She was also a founding member of An Óige, the Irish youth hostelling organisation and in this photograph, taken in 1956, she is seen at the opening of the Mountshannon youth hostel in Co Clare. She is to the right of the clergyman. Among her close friends were many actors, artists and writers. She also kept a big secret for many years, the relationship that she had. She and her partner never married, because if she had got married, she would have had to leave her job in the public service. The antiquated legislation that prevented married women working in the public service wasn' t repealed until 1973.

Thekla Beere died in 1991 and her funeral service took place at St Brigid's church, Stillorgan.

Maurice Pratt

Maurice Pratt was for many years, the face of the Quinnsworth supermarket group, now Tesco Ireland. When he worked on the marketing side of Quinnsworth, before he became managing director, he always fronted the company' s television commercials, becoming one of the best- known personalities on Irish television in the late 1980s and early 1990s. He became renowned for his catchphrase: "that' s real value". After Tesco took over Quinnsworth in 1997, Maurice stayed for a comparatively short time to help see through the transition, before leaving to head up the Cantrell & Cochrane group. He is still very actively involved with many other leading companies in Ireland, including the Brown Thomas department store in Dublin, where he is a director, one of many directorships he holds. He also heads up the organisation for the tourism industry in Ireland, as chair of the Irish Tourism Industry Confederation.

When Maurice was in his early teens at St Benildus College in Stillorgan, in 1968, he played in the St Benildus GAA under 14 team, in 1968.

Opening of the Money Doctor Doctor with John Lowe, founder, far left, in 2000

John Lowe has been involved in the provision of financial services in Stillorgan for many years. He joined the Bank of Ireland in 1972 and spent many years working at its branch in the Stillorgan shopping centre. When that branch opened in 1966, it was the first bank branch in a shopping centre and it also became the location for Ireland' s first ATM or "hole in the wall" machine. John stayed with the Bank of Ireland until 1983 when he joined the old First National Building Society, becoming manager of its branch on the Lower Kilmacud Road. Then in 1999, he set up his own financial services and advice firm, Providence Finance services, trading as the Money Doctor, based on the Lower Kilmacud Road, where it has been going strong ever since.

A linchpin of the Money Doctor services in Stillorgan is Stephanie Cahilll, who has been the office manager for 20 years.

The Lower Kilmacud Road, pictured in 1972, long before the many retail developments along that stretch of road, complete with the long- gone Kilmacud Stores.

John Lowe

Every year, John Lowe, who makes many financial advice contributions to the media, publishes an enormous book on the subject, immensely useful for consumers. He is seen here on the golf course, with a copy of his 2016 epic book in the foreground.

C & D Shoes

C & D Shoes is one of the few retailers in the Stillorgan Village shopping centre to have been there since its inception in 1966. The shop is run by Trevor Jackman and Anthony Hughes and in addition to shoe repairs, it has expanded in all kinds of ancilliary areas, like key cutting.

Stillorgan retailers

Diffney's mens' outfitters is a comparative newcomer to the Stillorgan Village shopping centre, where its shop sells a wide variety of high quality mens' fashions. The firm dates back to 1949, but it only opened in the shopping centre 15 years ago.

Donnybrook Fair and Tesco extension, 2017

Donnybrook Fair, which is headquartered on Morehampton Road in Donnybrook, has expanded considerably in recent years, under the guidance of its owner, Joe Doyle, including to the Stillorgan shopping centre in 2011. There, its store faces the Lower Kilmacud Road. The store has a wide variety of sections, including charcuterie, a craft butcher's, a fishmongers, a fruit and vegetable section and an off licence. Its many specialities include an extensive variety of ready prepared main course dishes and desserts. The Donnybrook Fair store in Stillorgan is said to be the best performing of all the stores in the group.

Close by is the big new extension to the Tesco supermarket, which was built during 2017.

Oatlands College

Oatlands College is a comparatively modern building, dating back to the late 1960s; it was built on the site of an 18th century house, also called Oatlands, which stood on about five hectares of land. In 1910, the house and its grounds came into the possession of the Darley family, who owned Stillorgan's famous brewery on Brewery Road. The last private owner of the house was Lady Jane O'Connell, who died in 1949. The following year, the house was acquired by the Christian Brothers for use as a secondary school. The old house lasted until 1968 when it was demolished to make way for the present college. Over the years since, many extensions have been made, including a new sports hall in 2012. At the back of the secondary school is Oatlands primary school.

St Brigid's church

There's been a school connected with St Brigid's church since at least the 1650s. The history of the school up to the later 19th century remains sketchy, but a detailed history of the school was written and published in recent years, covering the period from 1862 to 1985. By the 1980s, the school building had got very delapidated, but a brand new school was opened at the end of that decade.

Granada

This fine house in the Spanish style can be easily seen from the nearby N11 road. Granada is part of the St John of God hospital in Stillorgan, but the house far predates the arrival of that Order in Stillorgan. The house was built in 1778, just over a century before the Order came to Stillorgan. For many years, this ornate house, with an exquisitely designed interior that includes finely designed rooms and staircase, as well as stained glass in the windows, was a private house. In more recent times, one of the Bewley family, Mrs Harriet Bewley, lived there from 1926 until 1948. She then sold it to William Ahern from Ballsbridge, who in turn, in 1956, sold it to the St John of God Order.

Since the Order was founded in Spain in the 16th century, the priest who was given the task of renovating the house, Brother Stanislaus Phillips, decided to give the property a decidedly Spanish appearance. Extensive renovations were carried out in 2017, but these didn't detract from its essentially Spanish façade. The house is used as part of the St John of God facilities. Photo: Dominic Lee

New road

What is now the N11, which bypasses Stillorgan village, was once a single carriageway road. Plans to upgrade this road began as long ago as 1950, when the old Dublin County Council bought land so that the road could be extended and form a bypass to Stillorgan village. In the 1950s, Ireland's first dual carriageway road was built, from the junction with Newtownpark Avenue to the church at Foxrock, but it wasn't until the 1970s that the dual carriageway road from Donnybrook Church to the junction with Newtownpark Avenue was completed. The present Stillorgan bypass was opened in 1979 and a plaque to commemorate its opening can be seen on the wall on the opposite side of the road to Byrne's pub at Galloping Green.

Stillorgan's old railway station

The old Harcourt Street to Bray railway line opened in 1854, although Harcourt Street station didn' t open until 1859. But the station at Stillorgan, just over five miles from Harcourt Street station, had opened in 1854. It remained open until the entire line was closed down in 1959. It took 45 years to reinstate what had been so hastily closed down by CIE and the new Luas Green line opened in 2004, with a brand new station at Stillorgan. The old station at Stillorgan was converted into a private house.

Between 1932 and 1949, Drumm battery trains operated on the line, a precursor of the electrically powered Luas trams. Another feature of the old line, which was converted from steam to diesel working in the early 1950s, was the Stillorgan Express. It did the non- stop journey from Harcourt Street to Stillorgan, for evening commuters, in exactly 11 minutes, a time that has never been bettered since.

The Grange, a fine mansion that once stood in Stillorgan
Photo by Michael Lee

The Grange was a fine mansion just off the main road at Stillorgan close to its junction with Brewery Road. Built in the early 19th century, the house was occupied by the Darley family from 1834 until 1890; they ran the 19th century brewery in Stillorgan named after them. During the 1890s, the house was owned by Edmund Trouton.

From 1900 to 1914, The Grange was occupied by the Lee family; Edward Lee, who had been born into a farming family at Tyrellspass, Co Westmeath, in 1853, ran a noted department store business of that name in Dublin. His department stores were in such locations as Bray, Dún Laoghaire, Rathmines and his native Tyrrellspass. He was renowned for being a good employer, with a strong social conscience.

From The Grange, the Lees moved to Bellevue in Cross Avenue, Blackrock, where they were eventually succeeded as owners and occupiers by Éamon de Valera and his family. Edward Lee died in 1927, his wife Annie in 1938. The great- grandson of Edward Lee is Michael Lee, who is the chief cameraman in RTÉ television; he compiled and wrote a book on the history of the Lee family, published in 2016. Photo Michael Lee

The old gate lodge at The Grange

Eventually, The Grange was demolished to make way for the new headquarters of Esso Ireland, which opened in 1960. After 40 years in Stillorgan, the Esso building was demolished and today, a range of apartments and offices stands on the site and appropriately, they are named after The Grange. The development on the site includes just over 500 apartments and more than 4, 000 square metres of office space.

During the time that the Very Rev Lewis Crosby was the rector of St Brigid' s church in Stillorgan, he lived at The Grange, between 1924 and 1940. He found that the rectory of St Brigid' s was far too small for his family needs, so he rented The Grange.

While The Grange was a large and finely proportioned house, complete with gate lodge, it also had extensive grounds, hidden behind a high wall. In the grounds were a dairy, a small boating lake, a tennis court and a croquet lawn. Typical Edwardian entertainment for the Lee family included afternoon tea in the garden, listening to the music of Sir Edward Elgar and Count John McCormack on their new cylinder gramophone. Edward Lee and his wife Annie were both keen gardeners and often won prizes at local garden shows for their produce.

While the Lee family was in residence at The Grange, a fairly substantial number of staff were employed, including a butler, who also acted as chauffeur for Edward Lee' s motor car; two housemaids; a cook and for a short time, a nanny for the Lees' youngest childem Patrick, who sadly died within months of his birth in 1906. Annie Lee also had a companion, Annie Cosgrave, who came from Co Wexford, who had originally worked for the Darley family. When the Lees took over The Grange, she worked with them for the rest of her life, until 1920, as much a family friend as a companion for Annie. Photo Michael Lee

Diarmaid Ferriter

Diarmaid Ferriter, now a distinguished history professor at University College, Dublin, and a columnist with The Irish Times, pictured as a member of the school orchestra at St Benildus College in Kilmacud, in 1988, when he was 15. He graduated in 1991 from UCD, gained his PhD in 1996 and became Professor of Modern Irish History at UCD in 2008.

One of the best- known contemporary historians, his main interest is the social, political and cultural history of Ireland in the 20th century. As an author and a television presenter, he has often challenged conventional attitudes on modern Irish history and he does the same with his often controversial weekly column in The Irish Times. To give a flavour of his style, in one of his Irish Times columns in 2017, he asked how Irish religious orders had managed to get so rich at the expense of their services to the community. Photo: Diarmaid Ferriter

Jarlath Hayes

Jarlath Hayes (1924- 2001) started his career by working as a designer in various advertising agencies in Dublin, before graduating to become one of Ireland' s most talented book designers. He also had a keen interest in typography and he created the Tuam Uncial typeface used on the credits for the Glenroe soap opera, which ran on RTÉ television from 1989 to 2001. He also had a major input into the design of the Irish euro coinage, launched in 2002.

He, his wife, Oonagh, moved into their house at Stillorgan Grove in 1960 and in later years, he had his studio at his home, where he worked for such book publishers as the Dolmen Press and the Lilliput Press. The Hayes' five children, one son and four daughters, grew up in the Stillorgan house. One of his great loves was his succession of border collies, all called Murphy, another was his boat, although he couldn' t swim and the third was the willow tree he planted in the garden when the family first moved to Stillorgan Grove. Jarlath was also a keen carpenter and made all the furniture for the family home.

Jarlath had a great sense of humour and loved demolishing sacred cows, in whatever form they took. The photographs show Jarlath in his 70s, the decade of his life when he was happiest and most creative, while another photo shows him with Cathy, his youngest grand daughter.

Old Dublin Road

The old Dublin Road, Stillorgan, pictured between 1963 and 1966, when all the properties on that side of the road were cleared to make way for the construction of the new shopping centre. Note the old telephone kiosk on the footpath and the two cars on the pavement waiting to be serviced at Rothery's garage. On the right hand side of the photograph is a partial view of the sign for the brand new Stillorgan Bowl.

Lloyds gift shop, Stillorgan, in the early 1960s, derelict before its demolition
Photo by Denis Dowdall

Lloyd's gift shop on the old Dublin Road in Stillorgan was owned by R. J. Lloyd. It was in business from the 1920s until it was taken over for the development of the shopping centre in the mid- 1960s. A similar fate befell Lloyd's second shop, run by R. J. Lloyd's son, Willie, which sold second hand furniture, household bric a brac and did repairs to radio sets.

Rothery's garage on the old Dublin Road in Stillorgan traded from the 1920s until the premises were demolished 40 years later to make way for the Stillorgan shopping centre. At the back of the garage was a large yard with a workshop and the entrance to this yard was beside the second of the Lloyd's gift shops, the one run by R. J. Lloyd's son, Willie. Besides being a garage, Rothery's also had a fleet of haulage trucks used for general haulage. During the second world war 'emergency', Rothery's trucks brought turf down from the Glencullen Bog in the Dublin mountains. The firm was nothing if not versatile; it also did bicycle repairs. Originally, Rothery's Garage had petrol pumps on the pavement but these had been taken down by the early 1960s.

Kilmacud Road in early 1960s

Old houses, long since demolished, on the Lower Kilmacud Road in the early 1960s, opposite the Ormonde Cinema. In the mid-1960s, many old cottages on the Upper Kilmacud Road, opposite the Kilmacud Crokes GAA club, were demolished.

Some of the staff at the OK Garage in Stillorgan in the early 1950s. The garage was owned by the late Dick Kennedy, who lived on Glenalbyn Road in Stillorgan and whose parents lived at Ulster Terrace, Stillorgan. The OK Garage was subsequently taken over by Esmonde Motors in 1955 and it closed down in 2008. The premises have been derelict ever since and redevelopment plans have yet to materialise.

Denis Dowdall, now of Arklow, Co Wicklow, has put names to some of the people in this photograph.

In the back row, fourth from the left, is the late Frank Plunkett, from Newtownpark, Blackrock. Fifth from the left, in white overalls, is the late Barney Greeves from Carrickmines. In the front row, first left, the late Paddy Kelly from Dalkey and next to him, the late John Connolly from Shankill. Photo: Denis Dowdall.

OK Garage

In the early 1950s, it was usual to put cars up on the hoist for servicing at the OK Garage in Stillorgan. Technical equipment in the garage trade then was very unsophisticated compared to present day technology.

Stillorgan Reservoir

The reservoir is the largest man- made construction in the Stillorgan area. The Vartry water scheme was started in 1862, to bring water from a new reservoir at Roundwood, Co Wicklow, to Dublin city. An 84 cm cast iron water main brought the water from the Roundwood reservoir to the new reservoir at Stillorgan, which was built on lands attached to an 18th century house in the area, originally called Rockmore, but later known as Clonmore.

In 1914, along with the gun running to Howth, a big consignment of arms was landed at Kilcoole beach in Co Wicklow. The plan was to have these weapons stored at Stillorgan reservoir, but armed guards had been posted there, so the weapons went instead to St Edna' s, the school founded by Pádraig Pearse at Rathfarnham.

In recent times, there have been three reservoirs at Stillorgan, called the 'ponds' by people who work there. But an €80 million upgrade by Irish Water is under way, which will see one giant reservoir built to replace the three existing ones. Stillorgan reservoir still supplies 15 per cent of Dublin' s water supplies, so it' s still a vital link in the water network. But the new reservoir will have one fundamental difference from the older reservoirs; it will be totally covered in.

Linden Castle

The original Linden Castle dated back to the earlier 19th century, but by the end of the 1850s, it had been unoccupied for several years. In 1862, Francis Kiernan, a businessman from Westmoreland Street in Dublin city centre, bought the unexpired term of the 150 year lease for £1, 210. Then in 1864, the Sisters of Charity, who ran the original St Vincent' s Hospital on St Stephen' s Green, used £2, 000 given by a benefactor to buy the property and converted it into Linden Convalescent Home.

This convalescent home existed for many years; the name 'Linden' came from the many linden trees in its grounds. It was at Linden that a former Taoiseach and a former President of

Ireland, Éamon de Valera, died, on August 29, 1975. He was in many ways the most notable and most influential Irish politician of the 20th century. Photo: Larry Dalton

The grounds of Linden Convalescent Home had many fine linden trees, from which the Home took its name. It was run as a convalescent home for well over a century, until the Sisters of Charity sold the house and its surrounding land, covering 3. 5 hectares, in 1997 to a property developer, for £8 million. The old convalescent home was demolished and the entire site was redeveloped with new apartments. The first of these new apartments became available two years later, in 1999.

The 1950s saw several heavy floods in the Stillorgan area, then largely open fields, as streams and rivers in the area burst their banks. December, 1954 saw the worst of those floods, when the old Dublin Road was flooded to a depth of two feet in some places, causing heavy disruption to traffic and public transport. The main road, now the N11, was completely impassable in many spots.

Peter Jankowsky,1982

Peter Jankowsky was one of the great creative people to have lived in Stillorgan over the years, highly original in his approach to everything. Born in Berlin in 1939, he started coming to Ireland in the 1950s. He had trained as an actor in Germany and throughout the 1960s, worked as an actor in that country. He settled in Ireland in 1971, when he joined the staff of the Goethe Institute in Dublin, teaching German. For many years, he lived at Linden Lea Park in Stillorgan with his wife, Veronica Bolay, a distinguished artist, also from Germany, and their son Aengus, who now lives in Wellington, New Zealand.

But there was much more to him than being an actor and teacher; he was also a writer, a translator, a broadcaster and a photographer. For many years, he contributed to Sunday Miscellany on RTÉ Radio 1, where he had the most distinctive voice of any contributor. His radio scripts were always considered absolutely brilliant by a woman who was a long time producer of the programme, Martha McCarron. The photograph here shows Peter acting in a TV series broadcast by RTÉ in 1982. The series was called Caught in a Free State and portrayed events in Ireland during the second world war. Peter played the part of Dr Hermann Goertz, the most senior Nazi agent to have been captured in Ireland during that war.

Besides having so many creative skills, Peter also had a holy horror of modern technology. He refused to have a car, never used the Internet or a mobile phone and wouldn't even have a television set in the house. When he cut the grass in his back garden in Stillorgan, he always used an old fashioned scythe rather than a lawnmower. Despite his attitude to modern technology, he and his family lived in a typically suburban bungalow in Stillorgan. Peter Jankowsky died in St Vincent's Hospital, Dublin, on September 17, 2014 and is survived by his wife and son.

Denis Devlin

Denis Devlin, who lived all his life in Kilmacud, was a noted diplomat and poet.

Born in Greenock, Scotland, in 1908, his Irish family returned to Ireland a decade later. His father became a manufacturer of sweets in Dublin and the family did well enough to live in Westbury House, now part of St Raphaela's School, until they sold the house in 1932 to the Daughters of Christ of St Vincent de Paul. Denis Devlin started work in the then Department of External Affairs before the second world and from 1940 until 1947, worked at the Irish legation in Washington. Then he became Irish High Commissioner in London and following the declaration of the Republic in 1949, he became ambassador first to Italy, then to Turkey. His family home was always in the Kilmacud/ Stillorgan area.

Besides his diplomatic work, Denis Devlin also became a poet of great distinction. But tragically, he died at a young age, in 1959, from leukaemia. Among his personal friends who mourned his loss was Éamon de Valera, then Taoaiseach.

Westbury House, where Denis Devlin grew up, is still there, in immaculate condition. It is still said to be haunted by the ghosts of some of the 19th century socialites who attended balls and other functions there. After the Devlins sold the house, it was taken over by the Daughters of Charity, who opened an orphanage for boys and a primary school on the site. The original entrance to Westbury House is now the present day entrance to the Stillorgan Wood housing estate on the Upper Kilmacud Road.

The Handmaids of the Sacred Heart of Jesus, a Spanish Order, took up residence here in 1971 and developed the school. The new secondary school building, close to Westbury House, was opened in 1986. Subsequent expansions included a new wing in the 1990s and an Astro Turf sports complex in 2008. In 2015, the school celebrated its golden jubilee, at the same time, adding more classrooms.

Old cottages by the main N11 road, close to the site of The Grange
Photo by Hugh Oram

Old cottages at The Grange, at the junction of the N11 and Brewery Road, Stillorgan. In 2017, these cottages were due to be demolished to make way for a further apartment development.

In recent years, many high rise apartment blocks have been built alongside this portion of the NII.

Leopardstown Inn

The Leopardstown Inn, just off Brewery Road, a modern pub, was long owned by Brian and Desmond Reddy, whose family connections with the licensed trade dated back to the 1750s. In 2015, the Leopardstown Inn was bought by Brian O' Malley and Stephen Cooney for €4. 5 million and they continue the long tradition of the Leopardstown Inn being both a pub and a bistro.

Shiels' houses

The main house at the Shiels' Houses, just off the top of Brewery Road. A total of 24 alms houses were built here in 1869 by Charles Shiels, a rich merchant from Co Down. He was widowed early in his marriage and he and his wife had no children, so he spent the rest of his life on philanthropic work, building alms houses that provided rent free accommodation for elderly residents. These were built at four locations in Northern Ireland, while Stillorgan was the only place in this part of Ireland to receive them. The development at Stillorgan included a Gothic clock tower, seen here, as well as a giant Sequoia tree at the entrance to the site. In 1986, the Stillorgan site was sold to developers, who refurbished the existing 24 alms houses and built new apartments on the adjoining Arkle Square.

The Gothic clock tower, with its elaborate architectural embellishments that is the main focal point of the Shiels' alms houses at Stillorgan. Even through the architectural integrity of the alms houses, and the clock tower, have been preserved, these days, the former Shiels' homes are hemmed in by much housing built in more recent times.

Westbury House

Westbury House, now part of St Raphaela' s School at Kilmacud. The house was built in the mid- 18th century for the Pilkington family, who were very wealthy from their property and shipping interests. The house was one of the most outstanding in south Dublin and before the surrounding area was developed, it had commanding views over Dublin Bay. During the 19th century, many elite people from south Co Dublin gathered for balls staged in the vast ballroom. Today, the house is still supposedly haunted, by the ghosts of the many distinguished people who danced the night away at Westbury House.

In 1920, the great house was sold to a sweet manufacturer called Devlin and the Devlin family lived there for a decade; one of their children was Denis, who became a renowned diplomat and poet. The Devlins sold the house to the Daughters of Charity of St Vincent de Paul, who moved in during 1932, Eucharistic Year. The nuns established a primary school there, St Philomena' s. It was followed, in 1966, by a secondary school.

The Daughters of Charity withdrew from the secondary school in 1971 when a Spanish Order, the Handmaids of the Sacred Order, took over. Then in 1977, Sister Raphaela Porres y Ayllon, was canonised, so the name of the school was changed to St Raphaela' s, which exists to the present day.

Entrance to the Carmelite monastery, Upper Kilmacud Road
Photo by Hugh Oram

The entrance to the Carmelite Monastery on the Upper Kilmacud Road, Kilmacud. The Carmelite Sisters bought Kilmacud Manor in 1881 and turned the mansion into St Joseph' s Monastery, which is still there today.

Kilmacud House

Kilmacud House was built in the 18th century and its resident owner, from 1791 until 1845 was a prosperous wine merchant called William Magee. The Carmelite Order, an enclosed, contemplative order, bought the house from William Fitzpatrick, well- known at the time as the author of popular books on Irish biography, history and current affairs. He gave the nuns a primitive altar stone used for celebrating Mass during penal times and this stone has long been one of the Order' s prized possessions.

St Laurence O'Toole's church

St Laurence O' Toole' s church at Kilmacud; this comparatively new church, built in brick to an imaginative design, was dedicated in December, 1969. The parish in Kilmacud had been formed in 1956. The clerical figure who presided over the opening ceremonies for the new church was the highly controversial Catholic Archishop of Dublin, Most Rev John Charles McQuaid. The first parish priest in the new church was Canon Harley. But in recent years, the congregation has decreased substantially, so much so that a firm of architects devised a scheme of plywood screens to reduce the seating capacity of the church.

Mill House pub

The Mill House pub on the Lower Kilmacud Road. The pub is one of the modern hostelries in the Stillorgan/ Kilmacud area. Apart from the drinks served in its bar and lounge, the Mill House is also popular for its pub grub, especially lunches on Sundays.

St Thomas's church hall, beside St Thomas's church, Stillorgan
Photo by Hugh Oram

St Thomas' s church, an attractive Church of Ireland building, just off the Stillorgan Road, opposite St Helen' s Radisson Blu Hotel, dates back to 1874, when it opened as a chapel of ease. It cost £750 to build and was used mainly by members of staff at the then big house of St Helen' s. For many years, only evening services were held on Sundays, but in 1897, in response to local demand, Sunday morning services began. The church, which was further extended in 1964, has 16 stained glass windows, one of which was created by Evie Hone. The church can hold a congregation of about 160. From 1956 until 1994, Canon Trevor Hipwell was the only rector of the parish. Subsequently, it was grouped with the Booterstown parish of St Philip and St James. The present rector is Rev Gillian V. Wharton, who was instituted in 2004; she also ministers to Anglican students at nearby UCD.

The parochial hall at St Thomas' s Church, built in 1941 and dedicated to the memory of Monk Gibbon, for a long a rector in nearby Dundrum. He was vicar of St Nahi' s Church of

Ireland in Dundrum and also of the Church of Ireland church at Taney for 24 years, until he died in 1935. His son, also called Monk Gibbon, who died in 1987, was often called the Grand Old Man of Irish Letters.

The attractive rectory at St Thomas' s, which reflects the Arts & Crafts style, like the adjoining parish hall, was built in 1952.

Tigh Lorcáin farm

The ground was cleared for the development of the Stillorgan shopping centre in 1966. Across the road were the old buildings of Tigh Lorcáin farm. Among the row of shops on the old Dublin Road, facing the shopping centre site, is the Nimble Fingers shop. Ironically, before the new shopping centre, this small row of shops was known as the "shopping centre". Also nearby was Boland' s pub- still there- with the land beside it still awaiting development at the time.

St Brigid's national school

School children from St Brigid' s national school seen outside the school, just over a century ago. The original school dates back to at least the 1650s; the first recorded schoolmaster was Thomas Hickes, active during that decade, when he was paid £120 a year, a very considerable sum for the time. It has long been said in Stillorgan that the notorious Oliver Cromwell stopped by the school in the 1650s to attend a prayer meeting for his soldiers.

During the 18th century, the school fell into disuse, but it was re- established about 1764. During the 19th century, many changes and additions were made both to the school building itself and the way in which the school was run. The lowest point in the school' s history came in the years immediately after the Second World War, when the school had little more than half a dozen pupils. But in the early 1950s, the Church of Ireland population of Stillorgan increased quite considerably, trebling to about 650. As this happened, the number of pupils at the school began to increase steadily. By 1957, the school had forty- one pupils and by 1971, seventy. A decade later, around 1980, the school numbers had gone up to around the one hundred mark.

But such was the pressure for space that even the ground floor of the nearby rectory had to be turned over to school use. A brand new school building was opened during the late 1980s, almost entirely funded by the Department of Education. It was the latest chapter in the story of Stillorgan' s oldest school.

The history of St Brigid' s schools in Stillorgan for boys, girls and infants has been well researched, especially from 1862 up until 1985. A group of people closely connected with the school researched and wrote the school' s history, even if its earlier periods remain less chronicled. The people responsible for the recent history of the school were Jessica Classon, Hilda de Nais (a former principal of the school), Michael Classon (a former principal of Newpark School, Blackrock), and Canon M. B. Taylor (a former rector of the combined parishes of St Brigid' s, Stillorgan and All Saints, Blackrock).

The Hill, Stillorgan as seen in 1908

This postcard view of The Hill, then the main, indeed the only street, in Stillorgan village, was taken as a black and white photograph, subsequently coloured. It shows a remarkably rural village, with only a handful of people walking along. Cullen's wine and spirits store can be seen at the foot of the hill; the premises subsequently became what is the Stillorgan Orchard today. At the far right of the vista is J. Byrne's shop.

Linden convalescent home

The verandah at Linden convalescent home, where patients could enjoy some fresh air, either in bed or sitting on chairs. Linden had been bought by the Sisters of Charity in 1864 and they developed the house into a convalescent home. It was there that a former Taoiseach and a President of Ireland, Éamon de Valera, died in 1975 at the age of 92. The Sisters of Charity sold the house and its surrounding land in 1997. The old house was subsequently demolished and apartments built on the site.

Burton Hall

Burton Hall was a fine 18th century mansion, built around 1730 by Samuel Burton. Subsequently, it had many distinguished owners, especially a branch of the Guinness family for much of the 19th century. Henry Guinness, who was born at Burton Hall in 1829 and who lived for most of his life there, had a prominent role in running the family brewery. He died in 1893, aged 64.

The Guinness family also had links with the Darley family, who ran Stillorgan' s old brewery for many years. During the civil war, 1922/ 23, unsuccessful attempts were made to burn down the house. Then in 1939, Agnes Ryan of Monument Creamery fame, bought Burton Hall. She and her husband, Seamus, had started the Monument Creamery chain of shops, including one at 25 Lower Kilmacud Road, but Seamus died young, in 1933. Agnes lived at Burton Hall until she died, at the age of 63, in 1985, long after the shop chain had closed down, in 1966. After her death, the St John of God Order bought the house. Today, the name of the house is also commemorated in the name of one of the roads on the Sandyford industrial estate. Photo: Larry Dalton

St Joseph's Home for Adult Deaf and Deaf Blind

This fine mid- Victorian building stands at the top of Brewery Road, near to the Sheils' alms houses. It was created in the mid-1860s so that poor, deprived people from Dublin could convalesce after hospital stays, rather than return immediately to their hovels and tenements. The building fulfilled this purpose for a century, until in 1964, it was taken over by the Catholic Institute for the Deaf, which changed the name of the home to St Joseph' s House for Adult Deaf and Deaf Blind.

Ravensdale

This fine house dates back to 1778 and for many years, it was known as Ravensdale. In 1954, the house was purchased by the St John of God order and in renovating the house, the architectural style of the house was changed to make it look Spanish, in tribute to the Spanish origins of the order.

For many years after it was built, the house was known as Ravensdale; it didn' t get the Granada name until it was refurbished in the Spanish style in the mid- 1950s. In 1926, the house had been bought by Mrs Harriet Bewley, one of the Bewley family, and she lived there until 1948. It was then bought by William Ahern, a businessman from Ballsbridge, who sold it to the St John of God order six years later. The Order itself was founded in Spain in the sixteenth century, so in tribute, the house was given a very Spanish looking façade. Inside the house, there are wonderfully designed rooms and staircases, with fine flooring and stained glass windows. The house is still used by the Order and in 2017, further extensive refurbishment was carried out.

The original castle here has origins that far predates any other stately home in the Stillorgan area. It' s said that the first version of the castle was built on the site of Wolverston House, the home of an Anglo- Norman knight called Desmond Carew, who in the 12th century, owned the entire Stillorgan area. Subsequently, the fortified manor house passed through many other hands but the present Stillorgan Castle is comparatively young, having been built nearly 270 years ago.

Stillorgan Castle was rebuilt in 1750; in its subsequenty heyday, it was the setting for many great aristocratic balls and other social events. In 1882, its owner, Henry Deane Grady, sold the great house to the Brothers of St John of God, who developed it as a house of retreat for the old and the invalid. The Brothers soon expanded the building; a significant expansion came in 1890, when a community wing and a chapel were added. On November 25, 1908, a spark from a chimney started a fire in the clock tower that engulfed the building. But within three years, the castle was rebuilt. In March, 1913, the foundation stone for the new chapel was laid. However, this reconstruction was the last major piece of building work that the Brothers did in Stillorgan for a further 70 years.

In 1977, part of the land surrounding the castle was acquired by Dublin County Council for the new dual carriageway; the gate lodge and the swimming pool were demolished and the railings were removed to the St John of God location in Islandbridge.

Glenalbyn House

Glenalbyn House became the headquarters for the Kilmacud Crokes GAA club and the present building bears little resemblance to the old one.

St Helen's

This fine house, with extensive grounds, was built as a red brick mansion in 1750. Its first owner and occupier was Thomas Cooley, a barrister and an MP for the constituency of Duleek,

Co Meath. In its early decades, the house was called Seamount, before the name was changed to St Helen' s.

For many years during the 19th century, it was occupied by the Gough family; the Right Hon Hugh Gough, who came from Co Limerick, had a distinguished career in the British Army. He and his wife Frances, Lady Gough, had a long marriage, 56 years in all. She died in 1863 and her husband died six years later, at the age of 90.

Some 20 years later, a statue was erected in his honour in the Phoenix Park. In 1944, the statue was vandalised, then in 1957, what was left of it was blown up. After Gough' s death, the house was occupied by his son, until 1895. Then in 1899, the property was acquired by Sir John Nutting, a director of the Great Southern Railway. From the mid- 1920s until 1988, St Helen' s was occupied by the Christian Brothers, before being sold that year to a property developer. The future of both the house and the surrounding parkland looked very uncertain, but a preservation order was placed on the house

Subsequently, the house was turned into one of Dublin' s most luxurious hotels, ensuring that the interior fittings were well preserved. Extensive apartment development was carried out in the adjoining parkland, but the gardens surrounding the hotel have remained intact.

Pollock family mansion

This fine 18th century mansion stood on five hectares of land, where Oatlands College is situated today. The spacious 10 room house even had its own observatory. Part of the land at the back of the house was used for a kitchen garden, which for many years, provided fresh fruit and vegetables for the kitchens of the big house.

The property came into the possession of the Pollock family in 1840 and they owned it for seventy years. Then in 1910, it was bought by the Darley family, who had owned and run, with a little help from the Guinness family with which it was related, the renowned Darley' s Brewery in what is now Brewery Road, Stillorgan. The last private owner of the house was Lady Jane O' Connell, who died in 1949. After her death, the magnificent telescope was acquired by the observatory at Dunsink, but when a fire swept through the observatory in 1977, one of the precious items lost in the blaze was the great telescope from Oatlands House.

In May, 1950, the great house was acquired by the Christian Brothers, who the following year, turned it into a secondary school. This lasted until 1968, when the great house was torn down and replaced by the present red brick buildings of Oatlands College

St Brigid's church

St Brigid' s is by far the oldest surviving building in Stillorgan, going back just over 300 years. But it takes its name from St Brigid, who had founded a monastery in Co Kildare in the fifth or sixth century. From that monastery, in the ninth century, missionaries came to Stillorgan, where they built a monastery on what is now the site of St Brigid' s. The monastery had a small wooden church. In those days, Stillorgan covered a much wider area than at present, taking in Mount Merrion and going as far as Blackrock and Seapoint. In the 12th century, the church in Stillorgan was attached to the church at Kill o' the Grange while in the early 13th century, it was granted to Christchurch cathedral in Dublin.

By 1500, the church at Stillorgan was in ruins, but in the 17th century the church was rebuilt; in 1660, the church at Stillorgan was described as being surrounded by trees, which is still the case today. St Brigid's church was rebuilt between 1706 and 1712, but by 1760, it was in such a bad state of repair that it had to be rebuilt, creating the church we know today. Further restoration came in 1812, although it wasn' t until 1881 that the rectory was built.

Over the years, St Brigid has had some well- known rectors, principally Canon Ernest Lewis-Crosby (1864- 1961), the last chaplain to a Lord Lieutenant of Ireland. He was rector of St Brigid' s from 1923 until 1938, during which time one of the books he wrote was A Short History of Stillorgan.

In much more recent times, 1978, St Brigid' s Church of Ireland church was amalgamated with All Saints in Blackrock and the rector of both is Rev Ian Gallagher. The graveyard of Sr Brigid' s is especially interesting; since the church dates from long before the disestablishment of the Church of Ireland in 1869, the graveyard was used for burials by Stillorgan people regardless of denomination.

Glencairn

This fine house, built in the late 18th century, had a notorious owner at the start of the 20th century, Richard Croker, a leading figure in New York' s Tammany Hall. Since 1953, the house has been the official residence of British ambassadors to the Republic. In 2000, an alternative site was found at Marlay Grange and Glencairn was sold. Then it was found that it would be cheaper to repurchase Glencairn than continue refurbishing Marlay Grange, so the latter property was sold in 2007 and Glencairn continues to this day as British diplomatic property.

In 1976, just after he had been appointed British ambassador, Christopher Ewart- Biggs was assassinated by the IRA, which planted a landmine that went off as the ambassador' s official car was driving along near Glencairn. He had been on his way to his first meeting with Dr Garret FitzGerald, the then Irish foreign minister. Currently, the British Foreign Office has extensive plans for improving the security arrangements at Glencairn.

New Island Books

Dermot Bolger and Edwin Higel set up New Island Books in 1992, as a continuation of Raven Arts Press which Bolger ran in the 1980s. New Island Books is based in Stillorgan and is claimed to be the largest independent publisher of fiction in Ireland. Since its inception, New Island Books has developed into a major publisher of fiction, by new authors, while it has also revitalised the careers of established authors. Its Modern Irish Classics series, launched in 2010, has republished many Irish literary masterpieces from recent decades. New Island Books also publishes non- fiction.

St Laurence O'Toole's church

St Laurence O' Toole' s church with Monsignor Val Rogers, who was made parish priest in 1981. He occupied that position with great distinction, until he retired in 1995, aged 75.

Canon Harley was made welcome at St Laurence O' Toole' s church, when it opened in 1969. He was the first parish priest and he served there until his death on January 13, 1981. He was succeeded in June, 1981, by Monsignor Val Rogers, who served with great distinction until he retired on his 75th birthday in 1995. Fr Michael Loftus succeeded him, being installed during a very impressive ceremony during the Feast of Corpus Christi in June, 1995.

Fr Loftus died in June, 2007 and was succeeded as parish priest by Fr Liam Lacey, who took up his appointment on September 15, 2007. Fr Tony Coote was made administrator of the parish in June, 2010. The old church in Kilmacud now houses Fruit World, a shop renowned locally and beyond for its fruit and vegetables.

When St Laurence O' Toole' s church in Kilmacud was dedicated on December 14, 1969, an elaborate ceremony was presided over by the very controversial Catholic Archbishop of Dublin, Dr Charles McQuaid. Local FCA (reserve) soldiers even mustered, complete with their rifles, inside the new church.

The Hill

An exquisite painting of The Hill, the original main street in Stillorgan, was done by Olivia Hayes and shows some of the shops on the street, which is punctuated at its top end by Boland' s pub and at its lower end by the Stillorgan Orchard pub.

Archbishop Whately

Archbishop Whately (1787- 1863) was beyond doubt the most eccentric archbishop ever appointed in Ireland. Born and brought up in England, he had no experience whatsoever of Ireland before being made Church of Ireland Archbishop of Dublin, an appointment he held from 1831 until his death.

His blunt manner, a complete lack of a conciliatory spirit and gross manners didn' t endear him to his fellow clergymen. His personal behaviour was often highly eccentric and this eccentricity extended into his conversations. He refused to live in the archbishop' s palace on St Stephen' s Green and instead, lived at Redesdale House in Kilmacud for almost 30 years. There, he was able to pursue two objectives close to his heart, walking in the gardens and grafting plants. Bryan MacMahon of the Kilmacud & Stillorgan Historical Society wrote a fine biography of this strange archbishop, in 2005.

Fiddler of Dooney

The Fiddler of Dooney statue in the Stillorgan Village Shopping Centre. The statue was commissioned for the opening of the centre in 1966 and it' s been there ever since. It' s the work of Imogen Stuart, a German- born sculptor, who has had a long career in Ireland. The statue shows four children dancing to the tune from the fiddler's violin and the work is placed in the main mall of the shopping centre. These days, exotic food stalls are often set up in the mall to tempt shoppers.

Ruth Ó Riada is seen with three of her children.

Seán Ó Riada was the composer and musician from Cork who changed the sound of Irish traditional music in the 1960s.

At one stage, he had been assistant director of Music in Radio Éireann, now RTÉ, and later became musical director at the Abbey Theatre. He went on to compose much memorable music, including the scores for such films as Mise Éire and An Tine Beo and he set up his own group, Ceoltóirí Chualann.

Between 1958 and 1963, Seán and his wife Ruth rented a house at Galloping Green, then in open country. The house was owned by the Byrne family, who still own Byrne's pub, which is almost next door. Every week, Seán would bring his group to practice at his house, followed by traditional dancing sessions on the bare floorboards of the living room. Eventually, everyone would adjourn to Byrne's pub for refreshments.

Seán Ó Riada died in 1970 at the young age of 40; his conspicuous consumption of alcohol did nothing to help his liver condition. Among his children are Peader, who is himself a distinguished composer and musician and Sorcha, who is a political correspondent with RTÉ television.

The old hospital building and chapel, St John of God's
Photo by St John of God's

The original hospital and chapel at St John of God' s, before they were burned down in 1908.

Old gates at St John of God's
Photo by St John of God's

In years gone by, the St John of God's hospital in Stillorgan had a large farm, which supplied the hospital with most of the food it needed, including butter, cream, vegetables and meat. By the 1990s, much of the land surrounding the St John of God facilities in Stillorgan had been built upon. At the time that St John of God's had its own farm in Stillorgan, around a century ago, the area also had many other farms. The best- known of all the farms in Stillorgan was Tigh Lorcáin Farm, which was located between what is now the N11 and the old Dublin Road in Stillorgan.

Edward Lovett Pearce

Edward Lovett Pearce, Ireland's leading neo- classical architect in the early 18th century and the person who designed the Obelisk in Stillorgan, came to live with his family at The Grove, just off the Old Dublin Road in Stillorgan. But his outstanding aechitectural career was brief; he died in 1733 aged just 34.

In time, this house was transformed into Tigh Lorcáin Hall, from which the renowned farm took its name. The farm managed to survive various road widening schemes, up to the early 1960s, then it was purchased to make way for the Stillorgan Bowl, which opened in 1963. Building the new bowling alley, which today is the Leisureplex complex, also meant demolishing the old Tigh Lorcáin Hall.

The old gates that once stood at the original entrance to St John of God's.

Stillorgan Castle

Stillorgan Castle, part of the St John of God's complex in Stillorgan, has a history going back far further than any other stately home in the district, since it was built on the site of Wolverston House, the 12th century home of an Anglo- Norman knight called Desmond Carew, who at that time owned the whole of the Stillorgan area. The present house, also known Mount Eagle, was built in the mid- 18th century. From then, for a further century, its great public rooms were the setting for many aristocratic balls and other social occasions.

Then in 1882, the St John of God order paid £4, 000 for the castle and converted it into a hospital. The entire building was destroyed by a fire in 1908, but was rebuilt within three years. The castle remains at the centre of the St John of God hospital in Stillorgan.

After St John of God's took over Stillorgan Castle, the order had great plans for a brand new hospital, whose plans are seen here. It remained an aspiration; this new hospital was never built.

Doreen Kirwan and Beaufield Mews

Doreen Kirwan, known as "Go- Go" because of her dynamic attitude, was married to Eddie (Valentine) Kirwan, a solicitor. She started off by buying and selling antiques and then she started serving her customers tea and home- baked cookies. She eventually turned the old coach house at Beaufield House into a restaurant, which opened in 1950. She was well- known in Stillorgan for driving round in her open topped Morris Minor, stuffed with her latest antique acquisitions. Today, the Beaufield Mews is still going strong, considered the oldest standalone restaurant in the Dublin area, if not the country. Beaufield House itself was derelict when it was set on fire by vandals in 1987; subsequently, Beaufield Manor was developed on the site.

The patio at Beaufield Mews in the 1970s. The field at the back of the restaurant was converted into a wonderful garden, one of whose uses was growing herbs for the restaurant kitchen. In the 1990s, the celebrated architect Alfred Cochrane designed an iron pavilion, which is still used for weddings and other ceremonies. The restaurant maintains many of its old artefacts, including the old water troughs for horses, the original arch entrances for coaches and the many items bought by Doreen and her daughter Jill. Today, the restaurant is still flourishing and newer facilities include the Loft Brasserie upstairs, used for evening meals.

Julie Cox, who runs Beaufield Mews in Stillorgan, with her late mother, Jill

Jill Cox, one of Doreen Kirwan's two daughters, took over the Beaufield Mews restaurant from her mother, and ran it very successfully for many years, as well as developing the antiques side of the business. Jill became a great expert on antiques and made many appearances on RTÉ television as an antiques specialist. Jill died in 2010 and the restaurant business was taken over by her daughter, Julie, who continues to run it today.

Orpen sculpture

A new and very imaginative sculpture of the Stillorgan- born painter, Sir William Orpen (1878- 1931) has been created by Rowan Gillespie. The Stillorgan Chamber of Commerce is one of a number of local organisations that contributed to the funding for the statue, which has been placed just outside the Talbot Hotel. Originally, it had been proposed for the Lower Kilmacud Road entrance to the Stillorgan Village Shopping Centre. The sculpture stands over three metres high and it has four sections, denoting various aspects of Orpen' s work, including his interest in nudes, and it' s topped by a sculpture in bronze of Orpen' s head.

Orpen, born at Grove Avenue, Stillorgan, and baptised at St Brigid' s church, quickly became one of Ireland' s leading portrait painters, depicting the great and the good in Irish society in the first three decades of the 20th century.

Byrne's pub in the old days

This photograph was taken at Byrne's pub at Galloping Green in 1963 and shows, from left: Gerry Byrne, the then owner, his sister- in- law, Edie O' Halloran, Gerry Byrne's wife, Una, and Larry Coughlan. Gerry and Una were the parents of the present owner, Ray Byrne.

Byrne's is one of the last traditional pubs in the Dublin area; it was founded in 1879 by Philip Byrne, great- grandfather of Ray Byrne, and today, the sixth generation of the Byrne family lives over the pub. The last major changes to the pub were made in the 1960s and today, it continues to have a delightfully cosy atmosphere. Most of the pub's trade remains local and it is less dependent on passing trade. Until the early 1960s, Galloping Green was still largely open countryside.

One of the pub's most famous customers over the years was Seán Ó Riada, the traditional musician and composer. From 1958 until 1963, they lived in a house closed to the pub and which they rented from Ray Byrne's grandfather. Photo: Anne O' Connor.

Baumanns

When Baumans became one of the first outlets in south Dublin to sell ice cream, a very popular new trade developed for the store and Jack Baumann took on many roles, including as an ice cream salesman.

Oatlands House

Oatlands House was built in the 18th century, on five hectares of land. It was a spacious Georgian house, with 10 rooms and its own observatory, complete with telescope. Part of the land at the back of the house was used for a vegetable garden. In 1950, the house and its land were acquired by the Christian Brothers, who opened a secondary school there the following year. The school in the old house lasted until 1968, when the big old house was demolished and replaced by the present college building.

The Hill

The Hill, Stillorgan, 40 years ago, with the Orchard at foot of hill and Boland's at the top. An earlier photograph shows the old Dublin Road in 1940.

Kilmacud House

Kilmacud House dates from around 1820 and was previously known as Belvoir and St Margaret' s. It' s adjacent to the Carmelite monastery on the Upper Kilmacud Road; the gate lodge, on the Lower Kilmacud Road, was demolished in 1960 and was close to what is now the site of the Mill House pub. Over the years, Kilmacud House had many owners. From 1949 for many years, the Sisters of Our Lady of Charity, used it as a home for elderly ladies. In 1996, the house became a refugee centre. In recent decades, the house has had many unsympathetic 20th century additions, including fire escapes. In 2016, the house was sold as a development opportunity and by 2017, all its windows were boarded up.

Kilmacud Manor

Kilmacud Manor is now the Carmelite monastery on the Upper Kilmacud Road.

The manor house, in its own extensive grounds, had been built in the 18th century. The house was extensive and was noted for its many social functions that drew members of the aristocracy from far and wide to Kilmacud. The property was taken over by the Carmelite Sisters in 1881. On November 19, 1881, seven Carmelite sisters arrived from their establishment at Roebuck and the following day, said the first Mass at Kilmacud Manor, which became St Joseph's Monastery. The next major development was the building of the chapel, started in 1896 and completed the following year.

The monastery became renowned for various crafts, including weaving, which continued until 1958, when it was stopped because materials were getting so scarce. It was also renowned for baking altar bread, while on its agricultural side, its vegetable gardens, its orchards, its hen houses and its greenhouses were also well- known in the locality for providing abundant fresh produce. The new monastery was opened in 2005.

Redesdale House

Redesdale House, which dates back to the 18th century, was marked on some older maps as Riddesdale House. In the 19th century, the notoriously eccentric Richard Whately, the then Church of Ireland Archbishop of Dublin, lived in the house from about 1830, for 30 years. Whately devoted much of his energies to the garden of the house and one of the famous personalities he entertained there was the famous explorer, Dr Livingston. At the end of the 19th century, the house became home to Sir Thomas Farrell, the sculptor.

In 1903, the house was renamed St Kevin's Park and for about 30 years, was a training school, before being taken over by the Sisters of Our Lady of Charity. It became the infamous St Anne's industrial school, known as "Girlsville". In the late 1970s, the house was bought by the St Michael's House group and it was demolished in 1998.

Beaufield House

Oliver Charles Plunkett was pictured at Beaufield House, Stillorgan, in the late 1880s; he and his family lived there between 1885 and 1888. The woman in the photograph is believed to have been his wife, Emma, while the group also includes his brother John Randal Plunkett. The identities of the other two men in the photograph are unknown. Oliver and John ran the family malting business in Dublin, Plunkett Brothers.

By the time that Doreen Kirwan, of Beaufield Mews restaurant fame, and her husband, Eddie, had bought Beaufield Mews in the 1930s, the house was derelict and they had plans, which never came to fruition, to turn the house into apartments. During the civil war, 1922- 23, the house had been a safe house for Éamon de Valera and his secretary, Kathleen O' Connell. Photo: Moya Hawthorn, great- grand daughter of Oliver Plunkett

Dr T.K.Whitaker

Dr T. K. Whitaker, widely known as Ken, was born in Rostrevor, Co Down but brought up in Drogheda. He joined the civil service in Dublin in 1934 and 22 years later, was made secretary of the Department of Finance, one of the youngest people ever to hold the post. In the late 1950s, he began writing his paper on Ireland' s future economic development strategy and this had a fundamental role in changing the Irish economy, indeed Irish society as a whole. After he retired from public service, he became governor of the Central Bank in 1969; also in the mid- 1960s, he became very involved in the cross- border co- operation that was just starting to develop. He also had a keen interest in the West of Ireland, which he frequently visited on fishing holidays. Married twice, Ken lived on the Stillorgan Road, close to the Belfield flyover, for 50 years. He died in January, 2017, at the age of 100, having reached his centenary the previous month. His house on the Stillorgan Road was sold during the summer of 2017.

Credit union

Stillorgan credit union dates back to 1967; it has now merged with the Donnybrook credit union to form the South Dublin credit union.

In 2008, the three founders of the credit union movement were immortalised on canvas by Jim Harkin. From left, they are Sean Forde, Norah Herlihy and Séamus P. MacEoin. At the unveiling of the painting were John Hume, a founder of the first credit union in Northern Ireland, in Derry, and broadcaster Marian Finucane, niece of Norah Herlihy. Séamus MacEoin, who was the manager of the umemployment exchange in Dún Laoghaire, had played a big part in founding the first credit union in this part of Ireland, in Dún Laoghaire and he then went on to found the Stillorgan credit union, in 1967.

A native of Kilkenny, Séamus had served in the army during the Emergency period of the second world war. After the war, he worked in a number of government departments, including the Land Commission before ending his career in charge of the employment exchange in Dún Laoghaire. A gentle and considerate person and a fluent Irish speaker, Séamus was totally dedicated to the establishment and growth of the credit union movement in Ireland, so it was fitting that when a branch was set up in Stillorgan, it was largely thanks to his dedication, as a local resident.

St Benildus College

The first students started at St Benildus College, Kilmacud, in 1966. The college had been founded that year, when free secondary education was started in Ireland and was named after the De La Salle saint, Brother Benildus, from Clermont in France. The first headmaster of the colleage was Brother Oswin Walsh. In its first year, the college had a mere 28 students, but by the 1967/ 68 academic year, that number had risen to 120. Fast forward 20 years and the college had 850 students. Although the college is located in Kilmacud, it serves a far wider area, including Stillorgan.

In 2016, on the 50th anniversary of its founding, St Benildus produced an excellent book detailing the college's progress over the years.

The college is on a 10 ha site, close to the Green Luas line. When the college started, the surrounding area was almost entirely farmland, whereas today, it's mainly housing estates. The college has a fine academic record with a higher than average number of students going on to third level studies. Its alumni include Diarmaid Ferriter, a well- known historian, Joe Lynam, a BBC presenter in London and Paul Cunningham, who has worked as a presenter and producer for RTÉ television for the past 20 years. Past pupils who had much sporting success at the college and went on to distinguished sporting careers have included David Gillick, an indoor athletics gold medallist, Derek Daly, a racing driver, Ray Cosgrove, a Dublin GAA star and Richard Sadleir, a former Ireland international soccer player.

Belmont House boarding school

Belmont House, at Galloping Green, dates back to 1790 and between 1833 and 1850, it was accommodated Belmont Boarding School. In 1863, it was taken over by the Oblates for use as a secondary school, which lasted until the first world war. But the Oblates continued to use the house until 1990; they sold off some of its land in 1987 for housing development, then in 1992, the house itself was sold. In 1996, the house was converted into Belmont Nursing Home, which still occupies the site. Photo: The Dublin Pictorial Guide & Directory of 1850

Old shops in Stillorgan

Conaty's began as a butcher's shop on the Lower Kilmacud Road in 1957. Today, the premises is used as a delicatessen and restaurant, run by the same family. Other fine purveyors of fine food that didn't last the pace in Stillorgan including Findlater's, which opened a supermarket in the Stillorgan shopping centre when it opened in 1966, but which only survived for two years, and the Monument Creameries, which had a branch at 25 Lower Kilmacud Road, Stillorgan. It was part of a chain of shops that were renowned for high quality bakery and dairy products, but the Monument Creameries closed down in 1966, just as the new retailing trend of self-service supermarkets was just starting to take off.

Old painting of Dublin Bay, as seen from Stillorgan

A remarkable painting of Dublin Bay, as seen from Stillorgan, was painted about 1820 by a well-known landscape painter of the time, John Henry Campbell (1757-1828). It's a remarkable vista, as it shows just a handful of cottages, some cows and an otherwise totally undisturbed landscape stretching as far as the shores of Dublin Bay. The upland area of the Howth peninsula can be seen in the far distance. The painting came to light when Whytes, a Dublin art auction house, sold the painting in 2003 for €4,000.

Belmont House boarding school

Belmont House, at Galloping Green, dates back to 1790 and between 1833 and 1850, it was accommodated Belmont Boarding School. In 1863, it was taken over by the Oblates for use as a secondary school, which lasted until the first world war. But the Oblates continued to use the house until 1990; they sold off some of its land in 1987 for housing development, then in 1992, the house itself was sold. In 1996, the house was converted into Belmont Nursing Home, which still occupies the site.

Jack and Catherine Baumann, far right, founders of the Baumann shop

Jack and Catherine Baumann (on the far right of this photograph) are seen with a group of their workers outside their store on the old Dublin Road in Stillorgan, almost adjacent to the Stillorgan shopping centre. Jack and Catherine started their business in September, 1947, and it soon diversified, including into delicatessen, a news agency, a builder's providers, hardware supplies and garden equipment. The ever resourceful Jack, known as 'the king of Stillorgan', also opened one of the first ice cream parlours in south Dublin. He often wore a white blazer and a bow tie and was noted for being an absolute showman, a talent he used for running many charitable events. Eventually, Val, the son of Jack and Catherine, took over the running of the business, right up to the present time.

(Back row l to r): George Maher Snr, Denis Dowdall, Mr.Traynor (Beaufield), Joe Larkin, Tim O'Brien, Kit McCann, Terence Durham, Mr. Lucks, Jack Traynor, ?, Eoin O Caoimh, George Maher Jnr.

(Middle row l to r): ?, Dick Nolan, Paddy Daly, ?, Michael Downey, Mr.Traynor (Beaufield) Kit Boyce, Bob Boyce, Hughie McCann, Mr. Lennox, Ned Traynor, ?.

(Front row l to r): ?, Tommy O'Byrne, ?, ?, ?, ?, ?, Paddy Hickey.(Officer in Charge), John Carroll.

(Kneeling l to r): Martin Lucks, Paddy Hickey's daughter, Joseph O'Neill.

Security personnel who served in the Irish Army in the Stillorgan area during the second world war.

Second world war 'Emergency'

This photograph shows a group of local security force personnel from Stillorgan being presented with service medals in the late 1940s. They had all served during the second world war 'emergency'.

Front row, left to right, includes Tommy O' Byrne, Paddy Hickey (the officer in charge) and John Carroll. In front of them, kneeling, are, from left, Martin Lucks, Paddy Hickey's daughter and Joseph O' Neill.

In the middle row, from left to right, Dick Nolan, Paddy Daly, anon, Michael Downey, Mr Traynor (Beaufield), Kit Boyce, Bob Boyce, Hughie McCann, Mr Lennox, Ned Traynor and anon.

In the back row, from left to right, George Maher senior, Denis Dowdall, Mr Traynor (also from Beaufield), Joe Larkin, Tim O; Brien, Kit McCann, Terence Durham, another Mr Lucks, Jack Traynor, anon, Eoin Ó Caoimh and George Maher, junior. Photo: Denis Dowdall

Enda Carolan

Enda Carolan was a much respected teacher at Oatlands College, where he taught geography for over 30 years. He was equally dedicated to the coaching of hurlings at the college. He coached many teams to success in various Dublin colleges' age groups and his most noteworthy success came in 1985 when Oatlands won the Leinster Senior Colleges' A hurling title and reached the All- Ireland final. He was also involved in the coaching of minor, junior and senior hurling teams with Kilmacu Crokes for several years. Due to ill health, he took early retirement and died in December, 2015. He is remembered by all who knew him as a gentle, shy and sensitive man who was a loyal friend and a great servant of Oatlands College.

Talbot Hotel

The present day Talbot Hotel is on the far side of the N11 from the shopping centre in Stillorgan. It's now a four star hotel, owned by a Wexford- based hotel company and extensions now under way at the back of the hotel will bring its total number of bedrooms to just over 200. The present name of the hotel is the third on this site. The original hotel, the South County, was opened in 1961 with a mere 26 bedrooms by noted hotelier, P. V. Doyle, whose other hotels included the old Berkeley Court, the old Burlington and the old Montrose. The South County subsequently became the Stillorgan Park Hotel, and then, the Talbot.

Stillorgan shopping centre taken over

After the Stillorgan shopping centre was taken over in 2015 by American property company, Kennedy Wilson, various designs were produced for the future refurbishment of the centre.

The Obelisk

The Obelisk, in many ways the symbol of Stillorgan, was built in 1727 by Lord Allen to help create employment in the area and also to commemorate his wife, Lady Allen, although she wasn' t buried there. The monument was designed by Ireland' s leading neo- classical architect, Edward Lovett Pearce, and built with granite. It stands just over 30 m high. When it was built, it was in opem countryside, but these days, it' s surrounded by housing estates. Close to the Obelisk is a brick built grotto, also designed by Pearce, which today stands in the back garden of a house in Stillorgan Park Avenue.

Pearce, who died young, in 1733, at the age of 33, had lived in Stillorgan at The Grove, which was subsequently renamed as Tigh Lorcáin Hall, which in the earlier 20th century was the centre of an extensive farm. The house was demolished and much of the farm land was used for the building of the Stillorgan Bowl, which opened in 1963. Today, the Leisureplex complex is on the site.

The grand house, close to the Obelisk, in which the Allen family lived, together with the surrounding estate, was eventually sold on to a succession of owners. The last private owner of the property was Marcus Goodbody, who was very friendly with members of the St John of God Order in Stillorgan. In 1923, he sold Obelisk Park and its house to the Order, for £4, 500. The house reopened the following year, 1924, as a geriatric facility, then in 1931, it was turned into a home for patients with learning difficulties. In the early 1950s, the house underwent yet another conversion, when it became a school providing vocational and other educational training.

View from Obelisk over Dublin Bay

The local history society for the Stillorgan and Kilmacud area uses a delightful photograph, taken from Stillorgan, showing the Obelisk and looking towards Dublin Bay, as the introductory image on its website. In ways, it represents a harking back to the painting created by John Henry Campbell in the early 19th century, when the area was almost entirely rural.

Mount Merrion House

One of the earliest stately homes close to present day Stillorgan, Mount Merrion House, built in 1711 as a new seat for the 5th Viscount Fitzwilliam. The Fitzwilliam estates were inherited by the 11th Earl of Pembroke in 1816. Mount Merrion House eventually fell into dereliction in the 1970s and was demolished in 1976.

Stillorgan comvalescent home

The Stillorgan convalescent home, a mid- Victorian building on Brewery Road, close to the Sheils' Homes, was designed as a place where poor and deprived people in Dublin could recover after being discharged from hospital. It' s now St Joseph' s Home for Adult Deaf and Deaf Blind.

Beaufield House

Beaufield House, close to the present day Beaufield Mews restaurant, was built in 1830. It was bought in 1850 by John Sweetnam, one of two brothers who owned Sweetnam' s long established brewery in Francis Street, Dublin. Eventually, the house was bought by the old Dublin county council and turned into flats, but in the 1980s, it became derelict. This photograph shows the front of the house in 1985, two years before it was demolished. In addition to the long vanished house, its two fine gate lodges are also long gone.

Findlater's

When the Stillorgan shopping centre opened at the end of 1966, one of the new supermarkets belonged to Findlater's, which had a chain of traditional style grocery shops in the greater Dublin area. Designs were prepared for the new style supermarket, but Findlater's only lasted two years in the shopping centre and soon afterwards, the entire Findlater's chain closed down.

Joe Lynam

Joe Lynam, brought up in Stillorgan and who had his secondary education at Oatlands College and his third level education at UCD, has worked for the BBC in London, as a senior business correspondent, for over 10 years. Joe's late father, also Joe, was show jumping correspondent for RTÉ in the 1980s and Joe is a cousin of another well-known cross-channel TV presenter, Des Lynam.

Before he became a journalist, Joe Lynam ran a chain of pubs in Germany and speaks fluent German. He now lives in London with his Estonian wife, Riina, and their two sons.

Jimmy Magee

Jimmy Magee, the legendary sports broadcaster, who lived in Kilmacud, died there in September, 2017, at the age of 82; his funeral Mass was at St Laurence O'Toole's church there.

Born in New York, he and his family came back to Ireland when he was a young child and he was brought up in Greenore, Co Louth. His first job was with the railway that once linked Dundalk, the Cooley peninsula and Newry, but within a few months of him starting work there, it closed down in 1951. But Jimmy had already made his first forays into sports journalism. He began his radio career working on sponsored programmes for Raidio Éireann, before becoming a sport commentator. His knowledge of sport was immense and besides being a commentator on so many sporting events at home and abroad, he also hosted sports quiz programmes on RTÉ television. Besides RTÉ, he also worked, in the 1990s, for UTV in Belfast and Channel 4 in London.

Children's House School

The Children's House School was started by Veronica Ryan, at Thornhill on the Lower Kilmacud Road. She had trained as a Montessori teacher at Sion Hill in nearby Blackrock and she also studied Montessori teaching in the Netherlands. She started teaching at Thornhill, her family home, with just six pupils. Then, a noted architect, Arthur Douglas, was commissioned to design a purpose- built school in the grounds of Thornhill. The remarkable brick- built building, seen here, was the first purpose- built Montessori school in Ireland, set in a garden full of trees and play areas for children. Even today, it remains a remarkable building.

Sadly, Veronica died from pneumonia at the young age of 45, in 1966, but the school carried on and has flourished ever since; it now has around 70 pupils. Beth Ann Doyle was the principal until 1968, then Madeleine Coen and Elizabeth Carberry took over as joint principals. When Madeleine retired in 2006, Micaela Kuh, the present principal, took over. She has overseen extensions of the school's work, both to its facilities and to its work, including the introduction of the 9 to 12 Montessori stage to the senior class. Today, the school continues to be the embodiment of Veronica Ryan's original Montessori vision for Thornhill.

Mill House pub

The modern Mill House pub on the Lower Kilmacud Road, named after a mill that once stood on the Kilmacud River, long since turned into an enclosed culvert.

Paul Cunningham

Paul Cunningham, who had his secondary education at St Benildus College, Kilmacud, has been working for RTÉ for the past 20 years, in a wide variety of roles on both radio and television, covering many topics at home and abroad. From 2001 to 2010, he was environment correspondent, while from, 2011 to 2014, he reported for the station from Brussels. He is now political correspondent.

Dermot Morgan

Dermot Morgan, a radio and TV comedian, was born in 1952 and educated at Oatlands College, before going to university. Between 1979 and 1982, he worked as a teacher at St Michael' s School, Ailesbury Road, while he was starting to make an impact as a comedian on RTÉ Radio. His talents found their radio zenith in the Scrap Saturday series, at the end of the 1980s. Subsequently, he had a very difficult relationship with RTÉ television and he had to wait until 1995 to get his big break when Channel 4 in London commissioned the first of the Fr Ted series. It ran for three years and the day after the last episode was broadcast in 1998, he died from a heart attack. Ever since, right up to the present day, the Fr Ted series has been endlessly repeated.

Glenalbyn swimming pool

Glenalbyn swimming pool was built in the late 1960s and for many years proved a popular venue for swimmers, both adults and children, as well as waterpolo players, in the area. But in January, 2013, Dún Laoghaire- Rathdown county council took the roof off the pool, saying it could be hazardous in high winds. The pool was then filled in. Since then, an interminable debate has been waged over whether the pool should be rebuilt in its exisiting location or in a brand new location. So far, little progress has been made towards getting a replacement swimming pool operational in Stillorgan.

Redesdale House

The great house of Redesdale, noted for its curved front, was built as a three storey house over basement about 1769. For its first 30 years, it was home to Sir Michael Smith, Baron of the Exchequer and Master of the Rolls. It was the largest house in the area and was noted for its big entrance hall and its wrought iron balustraded staircase. From 1837 until 1859, it was home to the decidedly eccentric Church of Ireland Archbishop of Dublin, Richard Whately. From 1893 until 1900, it was occupied by Sir Thomas Farrell, sculptor and then president of the Royal Hibernian Academy. It ceased to be a residential property in 1093 when the Catholic church bought it as a rest home. In 1916, it became St Kevin's training school, then from 1944 until 1973,it was the notorious St Anne's industrial school, popularly known as Girlsville. In 1976, the house was taken over by the St Michael' s House group and it was eventually demolished in 1998. The lands were subsequently built over with a new housing estate.

Glenalbyn House

Glenalbyn is one of the smaller grand mansions in the Kilmacud and Stillorgan area; it dates back to at least the early 19th century. The house was built on the old Carysfort estates in the Stillorgan area. Glenalbyn was originally called Jane Ville. In the old days, a small bridge near the house spanned Daly's River, which flowed beside Upper Kilmacud Road and which was subsequently culverted.

In 1912, Glenalbyn was bought by a man called Wilkinson, a well-known cattle dealer; the Wilkinson family lived in the house until 1962, when it was bought by a German, Captain Hartman. At the time, the Kilmacud GAA club, now the Kilmacud Crokes, was looking for land for playing fields and the club made him an offer for about 2. 5 hectares of the adjoining pasture land. The sale went ahead and shortly afterwards, Captain Hartman decided to sell the rest of the estate, as well as Glenalbyn House. The GAA club bought the land and the house in 1965, for just over £30, 000. The house went into use the following year as a community centre and home to the local GAA club. The tennis courts in the grounds also continue in use to this day, helped by the flood lighting. Many other games, pastimes and community activities are pursued in the house. A substantial functions room was added in 1981.

However, the swimming pool, just over 33 metres long, built in 1973, didn't last the pace. It was closed in 2013 for health and safety reasons, as the roof became unsafe. Ever since, controversy has raged as to whether the pool should be refurbished and reopened, or whether a brand new pool should be opened. Despite endless discussions and controversy, a new swimming pool for the area seems as far away as ever.

The Glenabyn tennis club, founded in 1965, continues to thrive, with about 260 adult members and about 160 children.

Maxine Jones

Maxine Jones is a former journalist turned stand-up comedian. She arrived in Dublin in 1990 to work for the old Sunday Tribune newspaper; from there, she moved to The Irish Times. Nearly 20 years ago, she launched a glossy magazine style publication for the Stillorgan area, Suburb; although it had a favourable response, it only lasted for nine issues. She went on to write a book about her experiences in Ireland, *Why are you here? An Englishwoman in Ireland*. She also has another claim to fame; she claims to have been Ireland's first divorcée, in 1996, after divorce became legal in Ireland.

In 2011, she found an entirely new vocation for herself when she did her first gig, in a Dublin pub, as a stand-up comedian. She says that working in the newspaper business has given her a lot of material and her new career has proved very successful, both here in Ireland and in Britain.

O'Dwyer's pub

O'Dwyer's pub on the Lower Kilmacud Road has had an extensive makeover in recent times, including the new Restaurant 118. At one stage, the O'Dwyer family owned both this pub and the Stillorgan Orchard.

At the beginning of 2017, Stephen Collins, a columnist with The Irish Times, who has close links with Stillorgan, wrote An Irishman's Diary about Eamonn Huff, the barman at O'Dwyer's, who was then about to retire after 43 years' service at the pub. Eamonn was brought up in the old Moore's Cottages, demolished to make way for the Stillorgan shopping centre. He and his family then moved to the far side of the dual carriageway, to the then newly built Patrician Villas, where bachelor Eamonn still lives.

During his years working at O'Dwyer's, Eamonn never resorted to a laptop or to social media, always preferring to converse personally with customers. For many years, he has also been noted for going to funerals in the south Dublin area, to pay his respects

Baumann's

From its earliest days, Jack Baumann was intent on diversifying, a tradition continued in more recent years by his son Val. Jack was often to be seen with a wide variety of goods displayed on the forecourt in front of the shop.

Redesdale

The great house of Redesdale, built about 1769, on the section of the Upper Kilmacud Road that runs from Kilmacud Road lower to the junction at Stillorgan Heath. In its time, the house had many occupiers, including the Church of Ireland archbishop of Dublin, Richard Whately and Sir William Farrell, the sculptor. In the earlier 20th century, it became a training school and then from 1944 to 1973, was St Anne's industrial school for girls, otherwise known as Girlsville. It was demolished in 1998.

The original Janesville, built around 1790, bears little or no resemblance to the present Glenalbyn, which is home to the Kilmacud Crokes GAA club.

Stillorgan shops and restaurants

The Golden Disc record shop opened a brand in the new shopping centre in Stillorgan in 1966 to complement its existing shops in Capel Street and Tara Street.

The shopping centre at Stillorgan, as pictured in the 1980s. Since then, the centre has changed quite radically and so too have the cars.

Ping's restaurant was once a high profile dining out location in Stillorgan, but it has been closed and derelict for well over five years now. Previous restaurants on the site included the Swiss Chalet, Blakes and Pappa Gallos. Although Ping' s had an excellent reputation as a high class Chinese restaurant, many local say that it never recovered from a high profile legal case taken against it 20 years in a dispute over the bill for a large party at the restaurant.

Ossie Kilkenny

Ossie Kilkenny, for long known as the accountant to the stars, including U2, can claim to be a son of Stillorgan, since he was brought up in an old house on the Lower Kilmacud Road that is now the site of the Décor Centre. But he and his family moved to Dundrum when Ossie was just six years of age.

In his subsequent career, he was financial adviser to U2 for 20 years, while his many other roles in the entertainment industry have included being the chair of the Irish Film Board and a director of TV3.

Aprile's

Aprile's has been a well- known Irish/ Italian eating out place on the Lower Kilmacud Road in Stillorgan for well over 50 years. In recent years, it has been much upgraded, to give it a cool, contemporary look.

Kilmacud Crokes

Members of the Kilmacud GAA Club in 1961 included Pat Sheridan, Billy Sweeney, Jody Sweeney, Larry Ryan, Frank Maguire and Sean Donnelly.

The launch of Peter Sobolewski's comprehensive book on the history of the Kilmacud Crokes GAA club, took place in 2012. Those at the launch included the late Tom Murphy, then club chairman; Micheál Ó Muireathaigh, renowned GAA sports commentator; Joanne Cantwell (RTÉ) and Peter Sobolewski.

At Croke Park in 1966, Crokes- Kilmacud won the Dublin senior hurling championship for the first time. Crokes Hurling Club was well established, but never won the championships. Then in 1966, the club amalgamated with Kilmacud GAA club and promptly did win.

The team was well photographed and included John Ryan, Eamon Rigney, Paddy Daly, Gerry Keane, John Cooney, mascot Niall Howard, son of John Howard, Mick O' Brien, John Maher, Mick Regan, —— Scally, Paddy Fox, Connie Walsh and Jim O' Neill.

Also there were the other team members, Jim Rea, anon, Micheál de Burca, anon, Kevin Houlihan, John Barry, anon, Mick Cooney, T. J. McDonnell, Ailbe McDonnell, John Moore, Brian Coughlin, Sean McDonnell, Frankie Coughlan, Dan Dunne, Dermot Cooney, John McCormack, Mattie Fox, Larry Ryan, Ciaran Daly and Ned Bermingham.

Nimble Fingers

In 2012, the 50th anniversary in 1962 was celebrated of the establishment of the Nimble Fingers shop on the old Dublin Road in Stillorgan. The shop had been started by Hilda and Robert Tweedy and the business was taken over in January, 1983, by Pat Staunton, following the Tweedys' decision to retire. The Staunton family still own Nimble Fingers.

In this photograph are seen, from left, Pat Staunton; Belle, daughter of Gareth Staunton and Gareth himself. His sister Katherine is one of the Staunton family currently involved in the business.

Pearce exhibition

The exhibition on Ireland's foremost neo-classical architect, Edward Lovett Pearce who had close connections with Stillorgan, ran in the public library in Stillorgan in 2013; included at its opening, in March, 2013, were Bryan MacMahon (Kilmacud Stillorgan Local History Society; Lyn Lynch; Pat Sheridan; Julia Barrett; Claire O' Connor; Anne O' Connor and Peter Sobolewski.

Ormonde cinema

The first Ormonde cinema, seen here, opened with a single screen in 1954. It was owned by an Arklow- based cinema entrepreneur, J. J. Kavanagh, who owned a total of 12 cinemas. The cinema was very modern for its day, but closed in 1978 because of declining audiences, due mainly to television. A brand new Ormonde cinema opened in 1983 in the Stillorgan Plaza. Even though this shopping centre failed after a few years, the cinema did quite well and it was expanded in 1997 into a seven screen multiplex. Further refurbishments came in 2011, after which the cinema reopened under the UCI brand. Subsequently, it became an Odeon and retains that name today.

Janeville

Janeville was a fine Georgian house on the Lower Kilmacud Road, built around 1820. It once had two gate lodges, one on the Lower Kilmacud Road, the other on Glenalbyn Road, both long since demolished. But the giant sequois tree just outside the front door still stands. The house had been built by George Tinkler, a paper manufacturer, whose premises were in South Great George' s Street in the city centre. The house was also surrounded by extensive lands, through which ran the Kilmacud River, known locally as Daly' s river. About 1886, the name of the house was changed to Glen Albyn and in 1912, it became Glenalbyn. The house, with 18 rooms, and its extensive grounds are now home to the Kilmacud Crokes GAA club.

Esso Ireland hq

The new Esso Ireland headquarters at Stillorgan opened in 1960, on the site of what had been The Grange mansion. Esso lasted at Stillorgan for 40 years and its headquarters there were in turn demolished to make way for The Grange apartments and offices.

Farmleigh

Farmleigh was a magnificent house at the corner of the main N11 road and Brewery Road in Stillorgan. It was built about 1820 and was originally named The Farm, being renamed Farmleigh in 1864. Thomas Jackson, who lived here with his family from 1923 until 1936, was married to Grace Orpen, sister of Sir William Orpen, the painter, who was born in Stillorgan. After the Jackson family, the house was occupied from 1940 until 1970 by Louis Werner, an optician, who got a mention in James Joyce' s Ulysses. Werner was the last inhabitant of Farmleigh, which was demolished the following year as part of a scheme to widen the main road through Stillorgan.

Baumann's

Jack Baumann was often seen with a wide variety of goods on display outside his shop in Stillorgan, which he had founded in 1947. He had been quick to diversify.

Don Conroy

Don Conroy, who was educated at Oatlands College and then the National College of Art & Design, has become a - known media figure over the years, by turn an artist, an environmentalist, a TV personality and a writer of children' s books.

Historical Society

The Kilmacud & Stillorgan Historical Society got going in September, 2001, and has been very active ever since in recalling and promoting the history of the Kilmacud and Stillorgan area.

In 2002, the founding committee included Bryan MacMahon, Anne O' Connor, Julia Barrett, Pat Sheridan, Clive O' Connor, Bonnie Flanagan and Peter Sobolewski. Committee members who have joined since 2002 included Lyn Lynch and Margaret Smith.

Bonnie Flanagan, the author of two books on Stillorgan, published in the 1990s, gave the society' s first talk, on Old Stillorgan, in November, 2001.Since then, the society has staged over 130 talks and has organised an annual outing every year. It has also published a number of books, including two by Bryan MacMahon. At the end of 2006, the society began publishing its annual journal, Obelisk, and in 2014, launched its new website.

Seán Ó Riada

Seán Ó Riada was the great Irish musician and composer, who completely transformed the approach to Irish traditional music. Among his many compositions were his scores for the films Mise Éire and An Tine Bheo.

From 1958 until 1963, Seán and his wife, with their growing family, rented a house at Galloping Green. It was close to Byrne' s pub and in fact the house (seen here on the right) was rented from the Byrne family. Ó Riada had started his renowned musical group, Ceoltóirí Chualann, which created a totally different approach to playing traditional Irish music. The musicians came out to the large house at Galloping Green once a week to practice. Seán Ó Riada also organised impromptu Irish dancing sessions; since these took place on the bare floorboards on the main living room, the noise level was dramatic.

After all these musical sessions, it was usual for all who had taken part to adjourn to Byrne' s pub for refreshments, although Ray Byrne, the current owner of the pub, says that there was no evidence at that stage of Ó Riada over indulging. Later in his life, though, alcohol addiction did become a problem. Seán Ó Riada was particularly partial to what he called "The Wedge", two glasses of whiskey, separated by a glass of stout.

Ray Byrne also remembers that Ó Riada often acted on impulse, as happened the day he came home to Galloping Green and announced without any prior warning, that henceforth the family home was going to become entirely Irish speaking. This presented a particular problem for Seán' s wife, Ruth, who wasn't fluent in Irish.

After the family left Galloping Green in 1963, they eventually ended up living in Cuil Aodha in the West Cork Gaeltacht. During his 30s, Seán Ó Riada began drinking heavily, which exacerbated his chronic liver condition. He died in a London hospital in 1971, at the age of 40, having led a tumultuous but intensely creative life.

Today, Peadar Ó Riada, himself a fine musician and composer, and one of the seven Ó Riada children, remembers vividly that when the family lived at Galloping Green, the whole area was in open country, with no housing estates or other developments to be seen. He remembers, too, that the bus stop was right outside the family house. He also recalls that since Byrne' s pub was so far out in the country, it could stay open all afternoon, whereas pubs in Dublin city had to stay closed. So Byrne' s became a great mecca for drinkers prepared to travel out from the city.

Road upgrade

Plans for upgrading the main road through Stillorgan lasted for 30 years. The old Dublin county council, now replaced by Dún Laoghaire- Rathdown county council, first stated making plans to upgrade the main road through Stillorgan in 1950. It bought land so that a bypass could be built. In the 1950s, the first stretch of dual carriageway in Ireland was opened, between Newtownpark Avenue and Foxrock church, but it wasn' t until the mid- 1970s that the dual carriageway was constructed from Newtownpark Avenue to Donnybrook Church. The present dual carriageway road bypassing Stillorgan village and going through Galloping Green was opened in October, 1979. A plaque commemorating the event is on a wall at Galloping Green, almost opposite Byrne' s pub.

When the dual carriageway was first opened through Galloping Green, so many customers' cars were parked out Byrne' s pub that they often took one lane of the new road out of commission, as it was being used for parking cars. But since that 1979 opening, there have been no subsequent improvements to the dual carriageway through Stillorgan and Galloping Green, even though the volume of traffic using the road has increased exponentially. The N11 starts at the top of Mount Merrion Avenue.

Public library

The public library at Stillorgan is in a single storey building in the St Laurence Park area, sandwiched between the old Dublin Road in Stillorgan and the main N11 road. It' s one of eight libraries run by the library service of Dún Laoghaire- Rathdown county council. The library first opened in 1975 and it was extensively refurbished in 2011, giving better access and more facilities for library users. Before the library opened, Stillorgan' s library had been based in the much makeshift conditions of St Brigid' s parochial hall.

Many houses in the St Laurence Park area, beside the library, have been boarded up for the past five years as debate has raged about where and when the Glenalbyn swimming pool is going to be rebuilt. Prominent local politicians such as Green Party TD Catherine Martin, have said that the alternative site for the new swimming pool, beside the Stillorgan library, was never a feasible option. Other local politicians have gone further, saying that the boarded up houses should be refurbished as part of the area' s social housing remit. So far, however, the houses have stayed boarded up.

Stillorgan Cycles

Peter McCann, whose family has long connections with Stillorgan, has two long established outlets in St Laurence' s Park. One is his Stillorgan Cycles shop, well regarded for the range of bicycles it stocks, while behind it is Peter McCann Motors, an independent car dealer with a workshop for repairs and service. The motor company also sells a lot of accessories.

His grandmother lived for many years in one of Moore' s Cottages, which were demolished to make way for the Stillorgan Shopping centre in the mid- 1960s. Peter' s father was born in that house in 1917. As for Peter himself, he started his garage business in 1976 and the bicycle business in 1979, making them two of the longest trading businesses in the Stillorgan area.

Stillorgan Grotto

The Stillorgan Grotto, on the old Dublin Road, at the top of St Laurence Park, was built in 1986. It' s a small grotto and the inscription reads "Erected by the people of Stillorgan, 1986". Ever since, it has been kept in good condition.

Baumann's

Baumann' s has been a retailing phenomenon since 1947. In the years since, it has expanded its services considerably, achieving many firsts, such as the introduction of an ice cream parlour to Stillorgan. These days, customers can choose from an enormous range of goods and services, everything from garden sheds to hardware, with many other products in between. Its latest addition has been antique vape rooms. One thing can be said about Baumann' s, it has never stood still in its quest to remain relevant to south Dublin shoppers.

Stillorgan College of Further Education

Stillorgan College of Further Education may look somewhat temporary, as many of its buildings are prefabs, but it has been an educational landmark in the area for just over half a century. It has been going strong as a centre for post leaving certificate and further education studies. It has state of the art facilities, including computer rooms, and a very high ratio of computers to students. Before the college was given its present name, one of its teachers was Dermot Morgan, who went on to win fame as a radio and television comedian. One well- known present day radio and television personality who undertook some of his education at the college was RTÉ's Derek Mooney. The college's most recent link up has been with the IADT college in Dún Laoghaire, renowned for its film making education.

The first principal, appointed in 1966, was Hugh McDaid, whose speciality was teaching woodwork. He retired in 1980 and was succeeded by John Sheehy, who spent nearly 20 years as principal, retiring in 1999. In turn, he was succeeded by Michael Carolan, who held the post for 13 years, until he retired in 2012. He was then succeeded by the current principal, Kevin Harrington. It's an amazing testimony to the college that in the space of 50 years, it has had just four principals.

Oatlands College

The brick built façade of Oatlands College, a voluntary Christian Brothers secondary school, has been a familiar sight in Stillorgan since the late 1960s. The new college replaced the old Oatlands House building, where the Christian Brothers started their secondary school in 1955. To the rear of the present day college is Oatlands primary school. Over the years, Oatlands College has been renowned for the sheer number of pupils it has produced who have gone on to have distinguished careers, including Dermot Morgan; Éamon Ó Cuiv, a grandson of Éamon de Valera and a prominent member of Fianna Fáil and Stephen Collins of The Irish Times.

Marino Branch
Brainse Marino
Tel: 8336297

Lightning Source UK Ltd.
Milton Keynes UK
UKHW031818240519

343284UK00010B/186/P

9 781490 793870